FOR ORGANS, PIANOS & ELECTRONIC KEYBOARDS

E-Z PLAY TODAY

146

DISNEP

THE LION KING

MUSIC FROM THE MOTION PICTURE SOUNDTRACK

ISBN 978-1-5400-6751-7

HAL•LEONARD®

E-Z Play® Today Music Notation © 1975 by HAL LEONARD LLC
E-Z PLAY and EASY ELECTRONIC KEYBOARD MUSIC are registered trademarks of HAL LEONARD LLC.

Visit Hal Leonard Online at
www.halleonard.com

Contact us:
Hal Leonard
7777 West Bluemound Road
Milwaukee, WI 53213
Email: info@halleonard.com

In Europe, contact:
Hal Leonard Europe Limited
42 Wigmore Street
Marylebone, London, W1U 2RN
Email: info@halleonardeurope.com

In Australia, contact:
Hal Leonard Australia Pty. Ltd.
4 Lentara Court
Cheltenham, Victoria, 3192 Australia
Email: info@halleonard.com.au

CONTENTS

Can You Feel the Love Tonight

Registration 3
Rhythm: 8 Beat or Pops

Music by Elton John
Lyrics by Tim Rice

I can see what's hap - p'ning. And they don't have a clue. They'll

fall in love and here's the bot - tom line: Our tri - o's down to two. The

sweet ca - ress of twi - light; there's mag - ic ev - 'ry - where. And

with all this ro - man - tic at - mo - sphere, dis - as - ter's in the

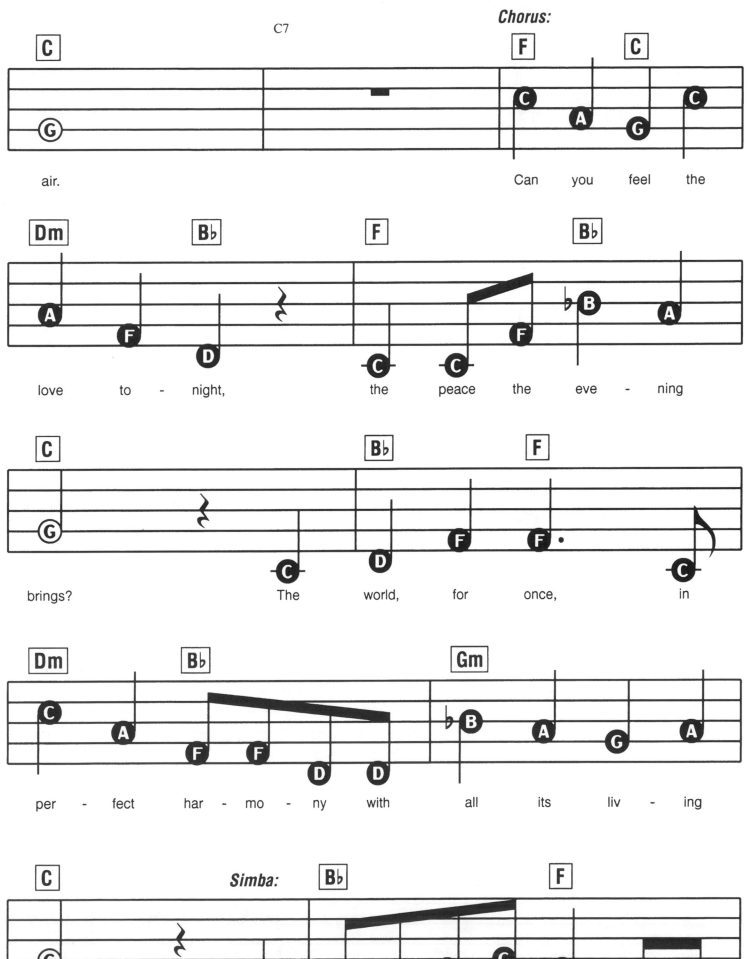

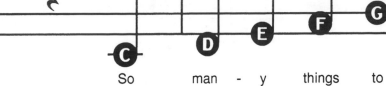

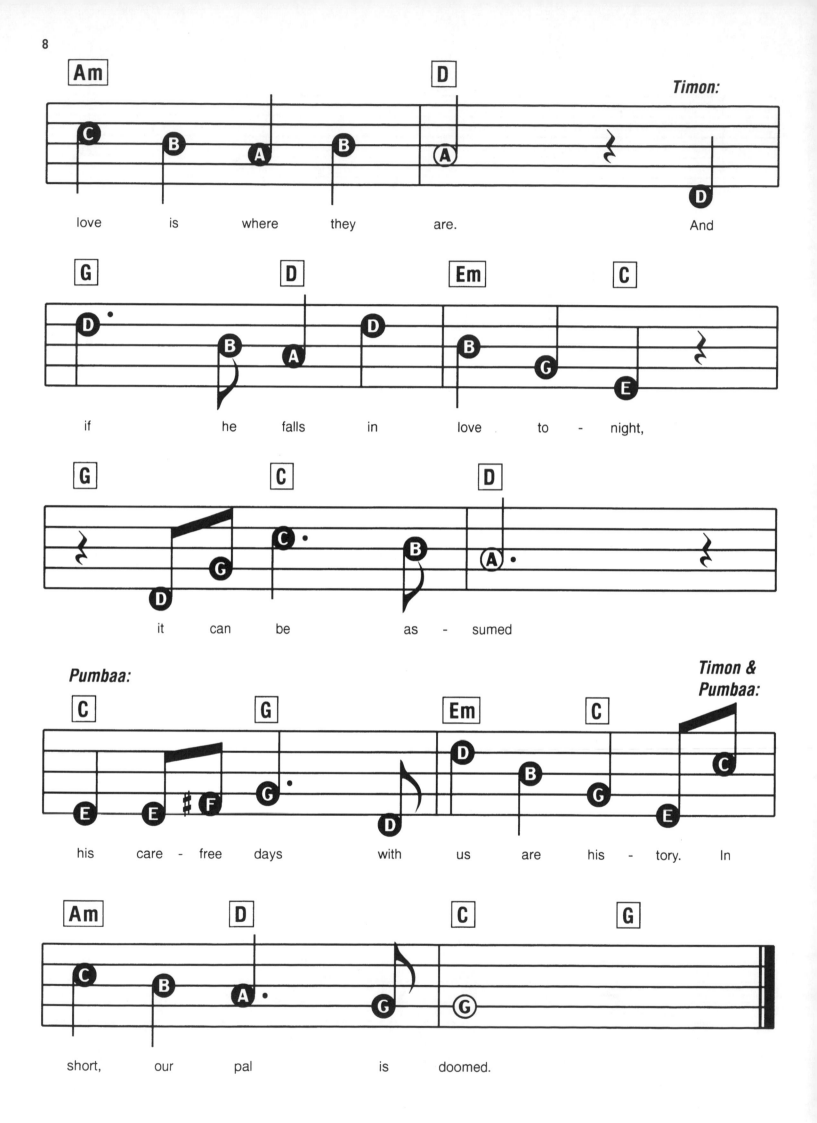

Circle of Life

Registration 2
Rhythm: Calypso or Reggae

Music by Elton John
Lyrics by Tim Rice

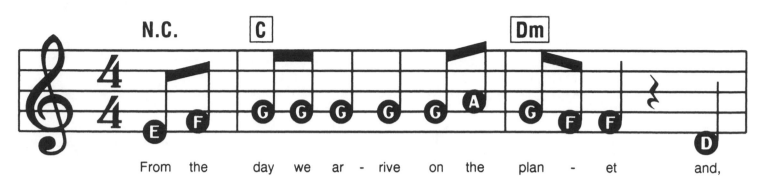

From the day we ar - rive on the plan - et and,

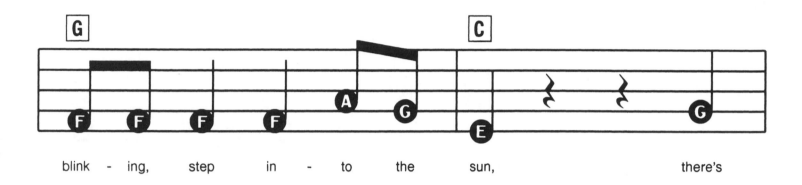

blink - ing, step in - to the sun, there's

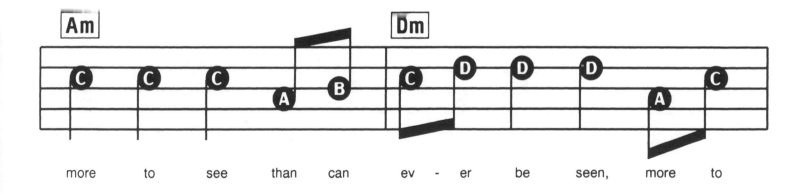

more to see than can ev - er be seen, more to

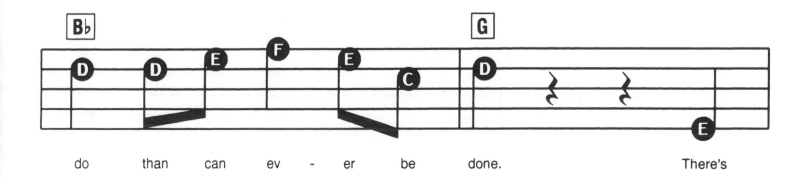

do than can ev - er be done. There's

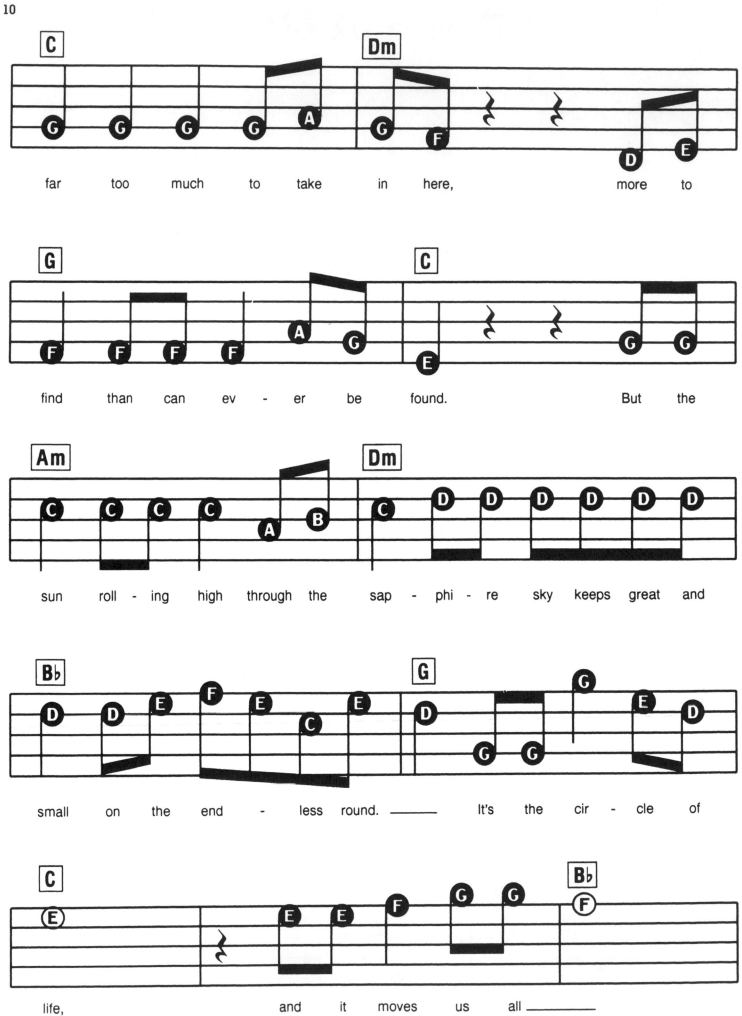

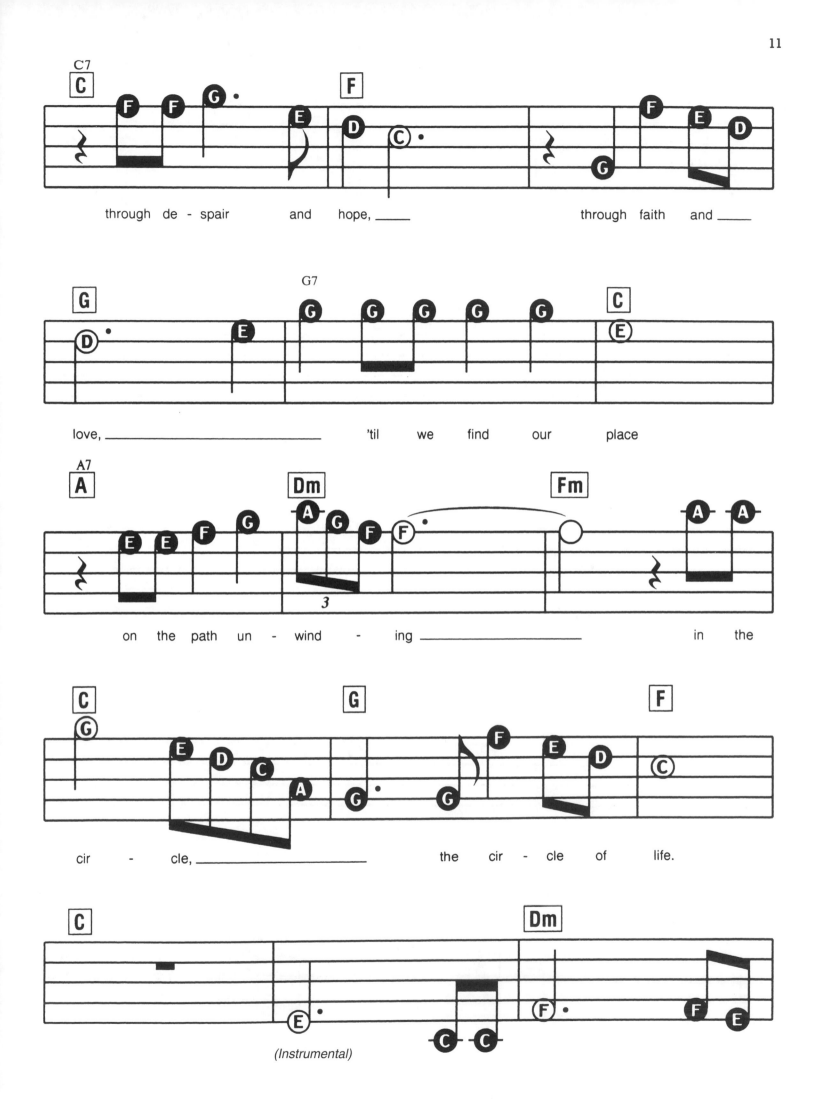

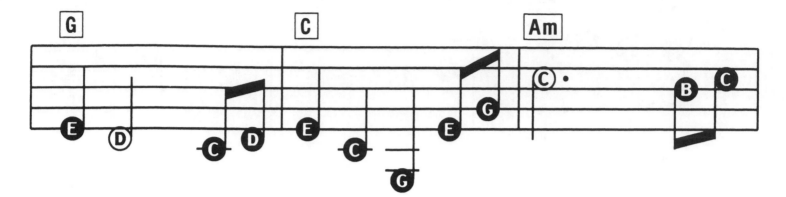

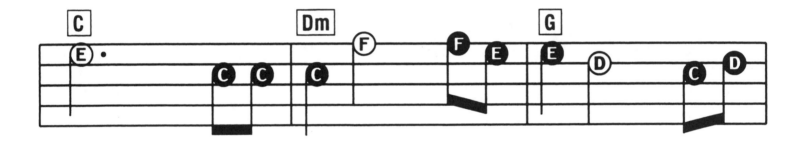

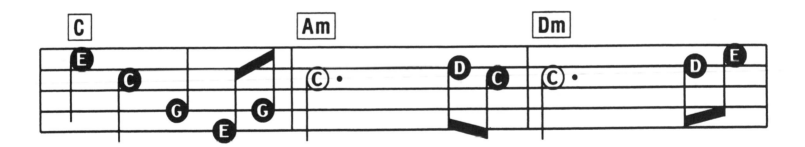

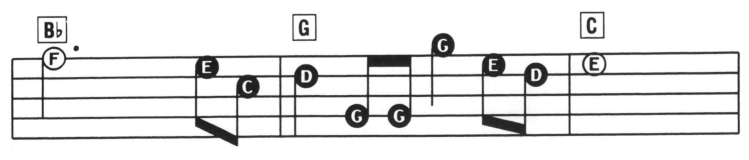

It's the cir - cle of life,

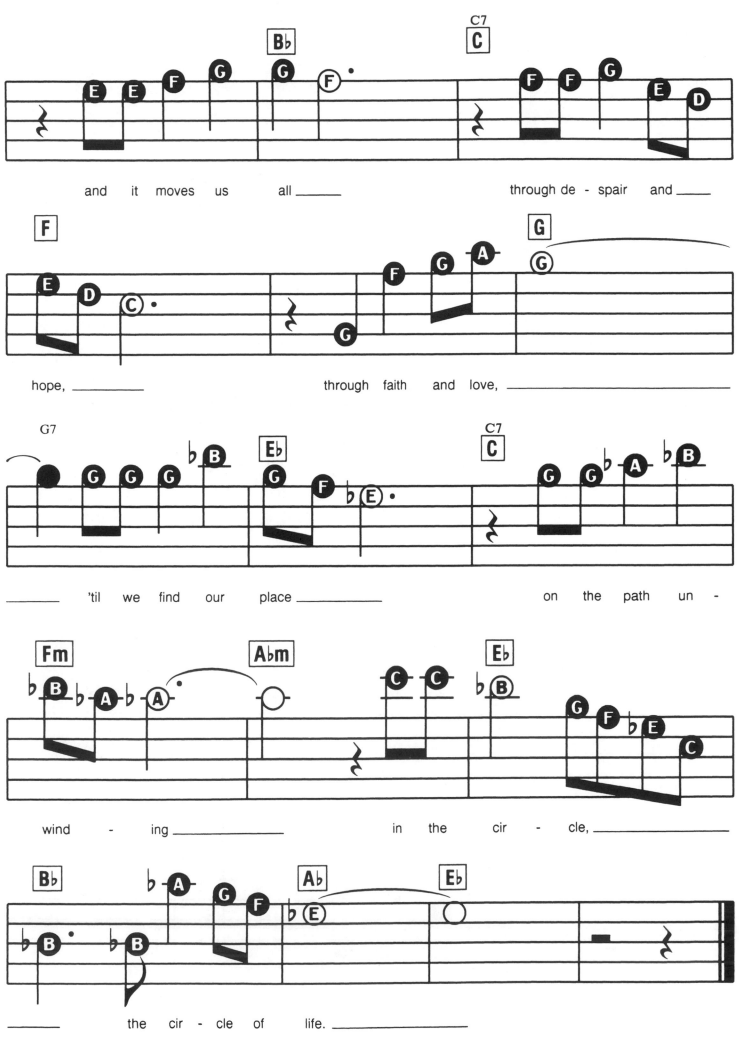

Hakuna Matata

Registration 5
Rhythm: Swing

Music by Elton John
Lyrics by Tim Rice

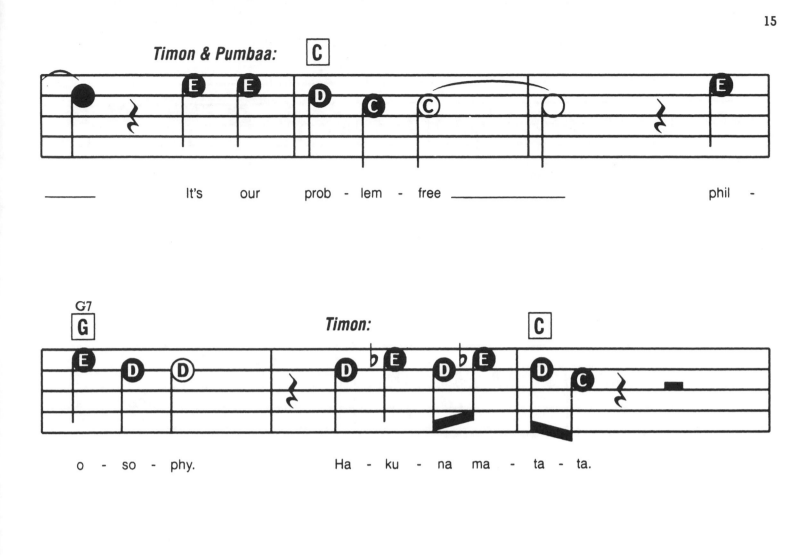

It's our prob - lem - free _____ phil -

o - so - phy.   Ha - ku - na ma - ta - ta.

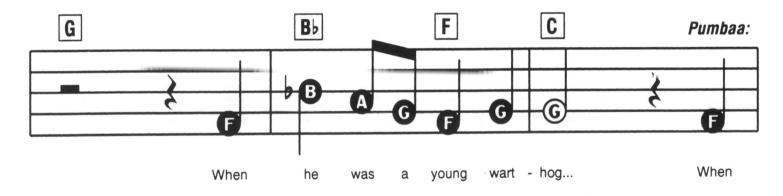

When   he was a young wart - hog...   When

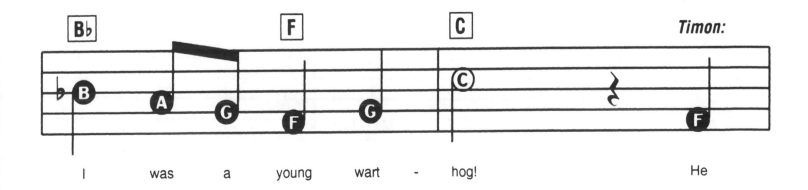

I was a young wart - hog!   He

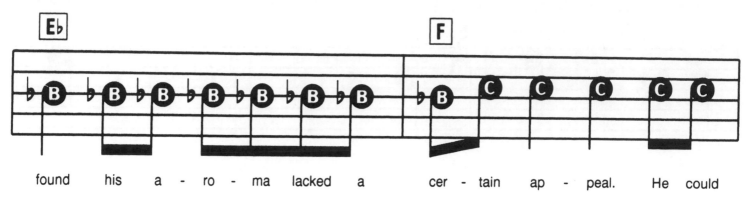

found his a - ro - ma lacked a cer - tain ap - peal. He could

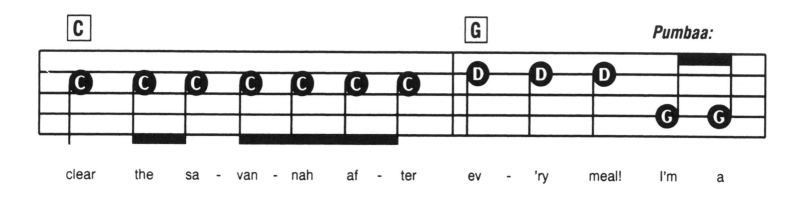

clear the sa - van - nah af - ter ev - 'ry meal! I'm a

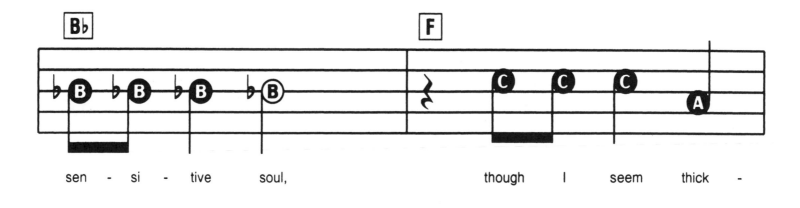

sen - si - tive soul, though I seem thick -

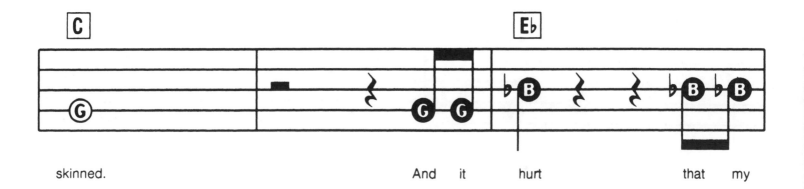

skinned. And it hurt that my

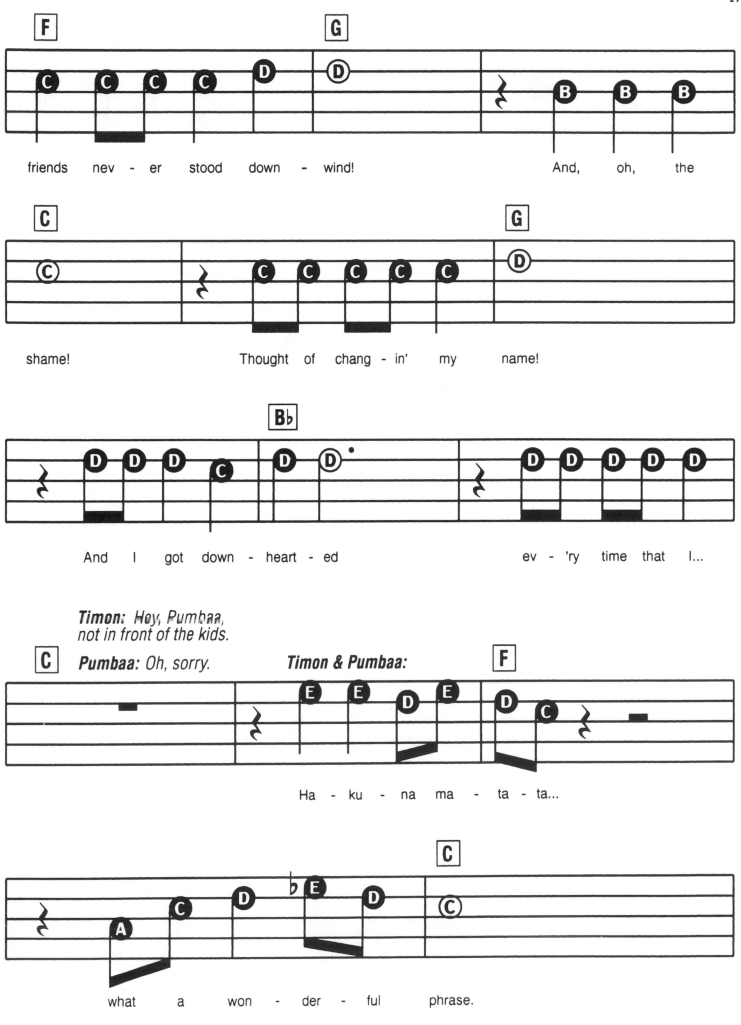

I Just Can't Wait to Be King

Registration 8
Rhythm: Motown or Rock

Music by Elton John
Lyrics by Tim Rice

far, a rath - er un - in - spir - ing thing. Oh, I

just can't _____ wait to be king.

No one say - ing "do this," no one say - ing

"be there," no one say - ing "stop that," no one say - ing

22

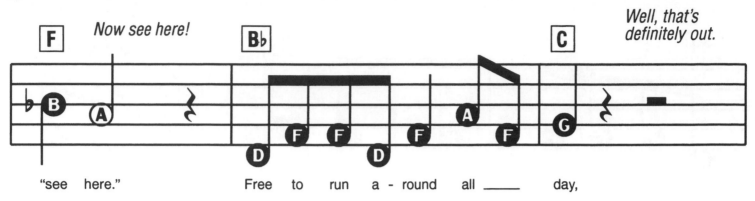

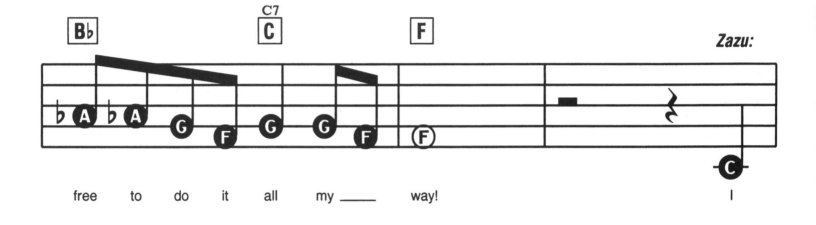

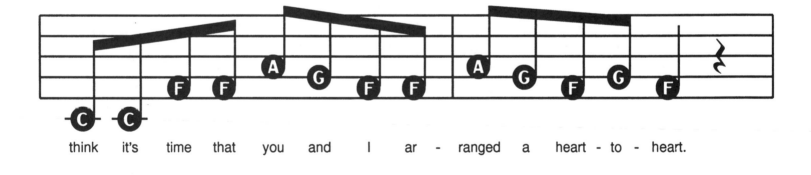

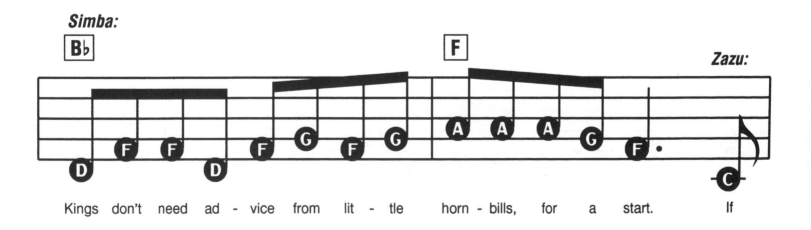

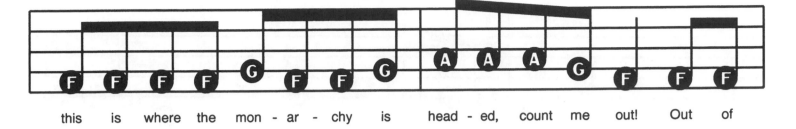

this is where the mon - ar - chy is head - ed, count me out! Out of

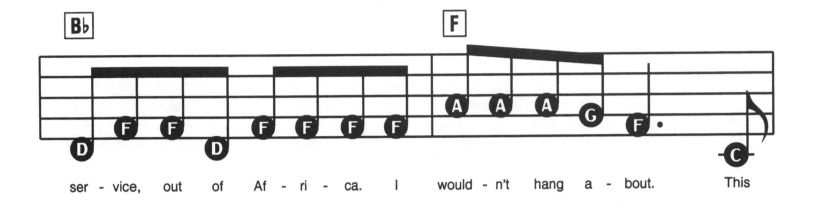

ser - vice, out of Af - ri - ca. I would - n't hang a - bout. This

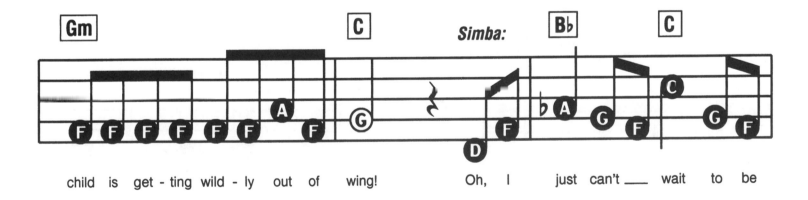

child is get - ting wild - ly out of wing! Oh, I just can't __ wait to be

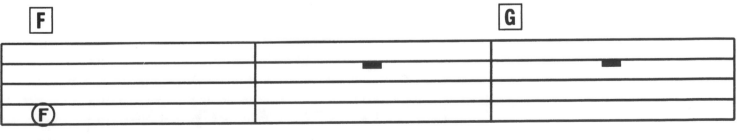

king!

24

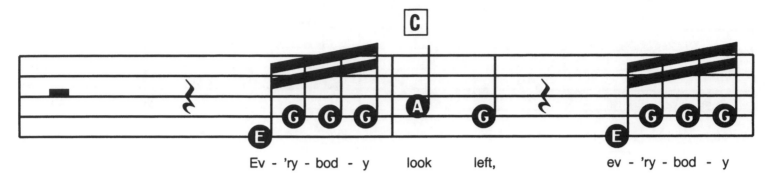

Ev-'ry-bod-y look left, ev-'ry-bod-y

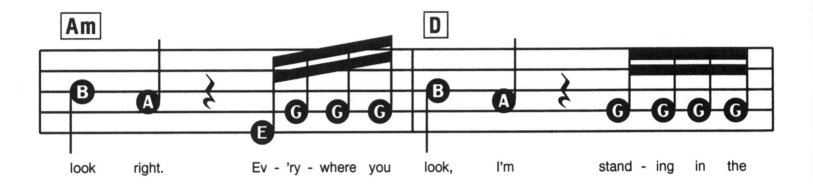

look right. Ev-'ry-where you look, I'm stand-ing in the

Zazu: (Spoken) Not yet!
Simba & Chorus:

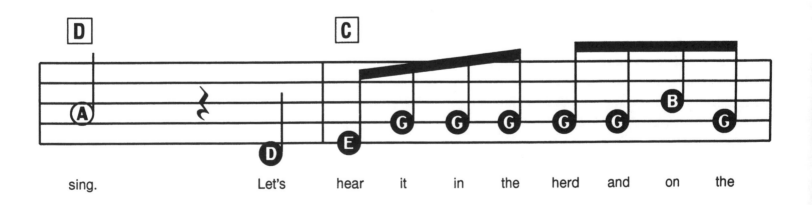

spot - light. Let ev - 'ry crea - ture go for broke and

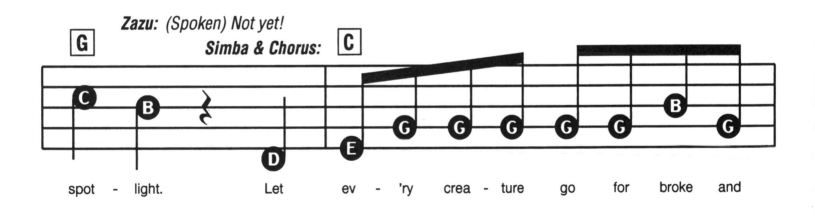

sing. Let's hear it in the herd and on the

Never Too Late

Registration 2
Rhythm: Pop or Rock

Music by Elton John
Lyrics by Tim Rice

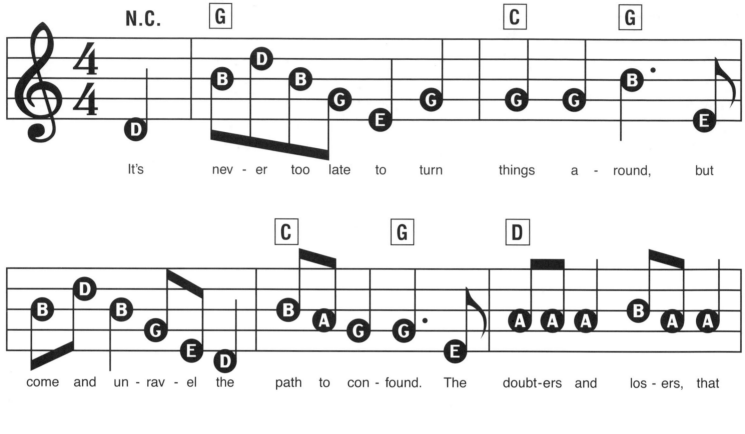

It's nev-er too late to turn things a-round, but

come and un-rav-el the path to con-found. The doubt-ers and los-ers, that

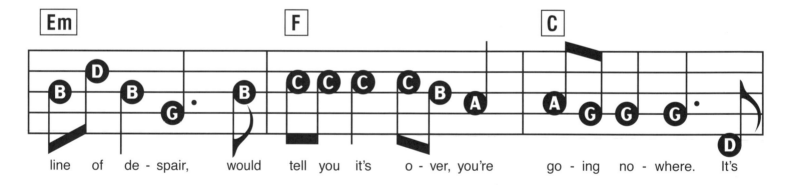

line of de-spair, would tell you it's o-ver, you're go-ing no-where. It's

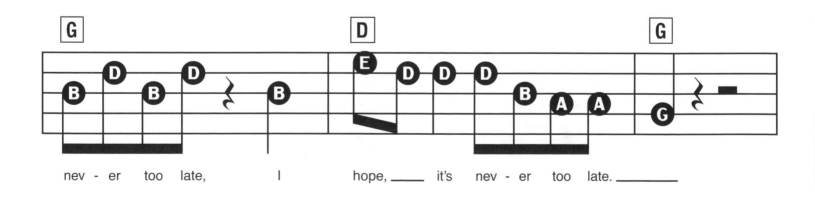

nev-er too late, I hope, ___ it's nev-er too late. ___

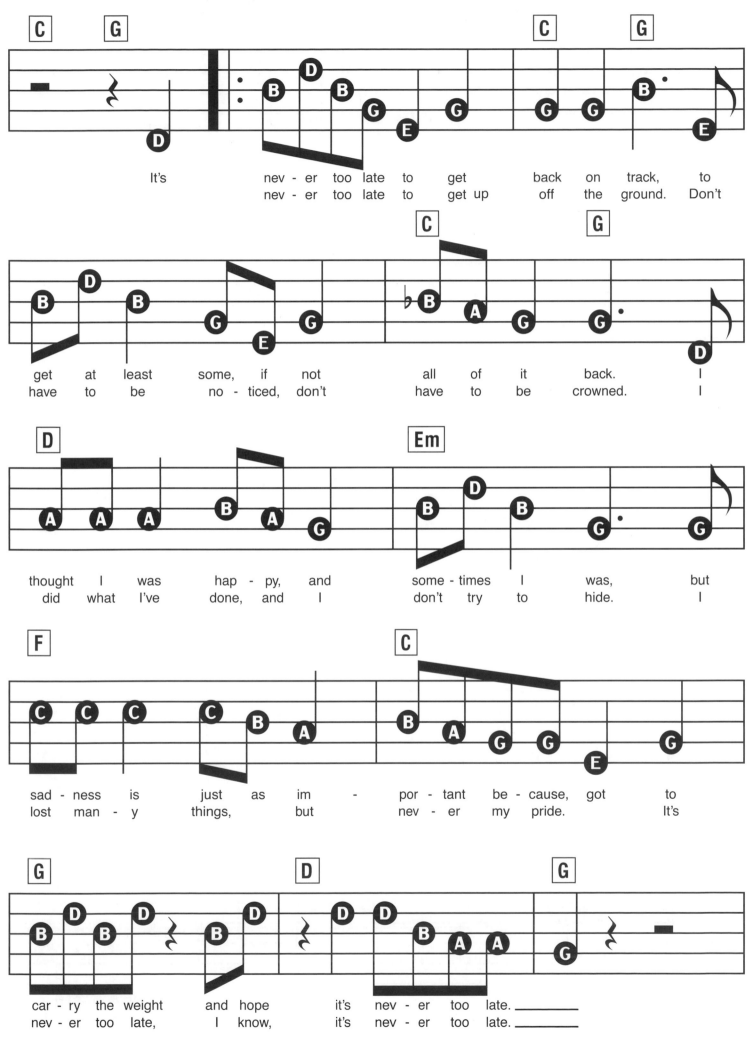

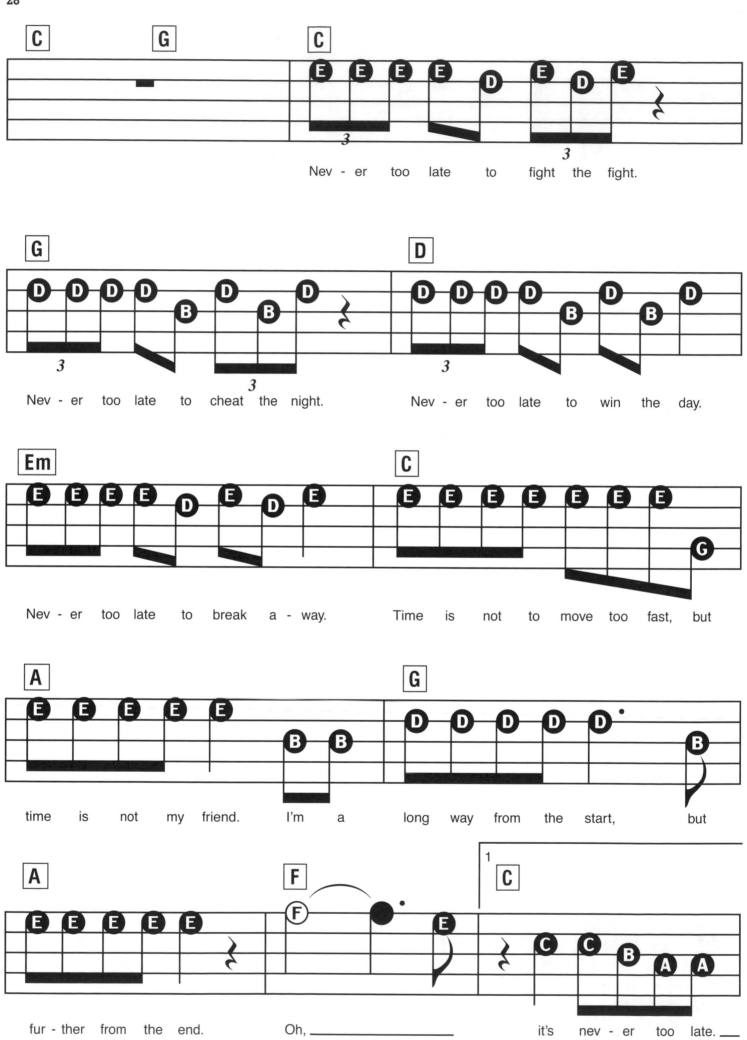

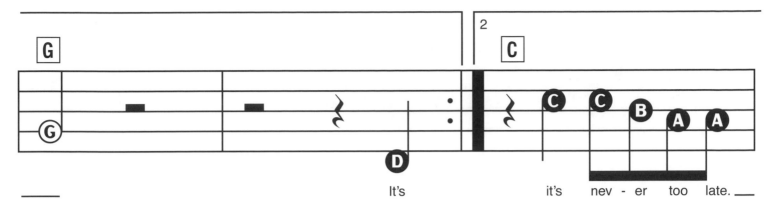

It's it's nev - er too late.

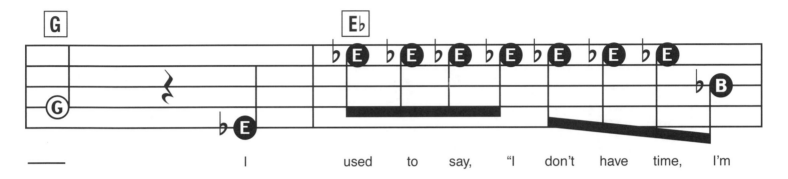

I used to say, "I don't have time, I'm

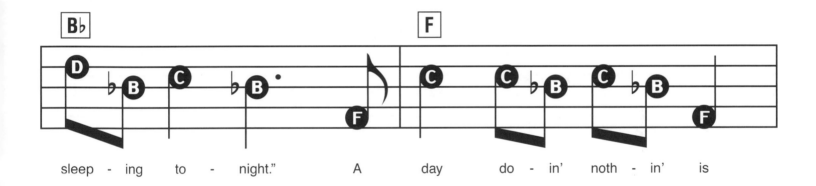

sleep - ing to - night." A day do - in' noth - in' is

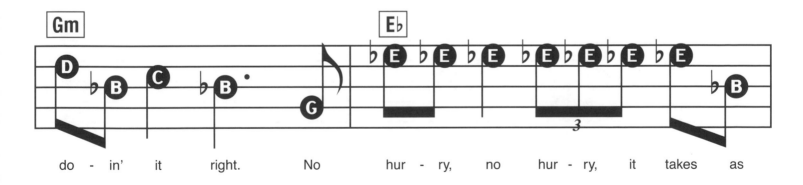

do - in' it right. No hur - ry, no hur - ry, it takes as

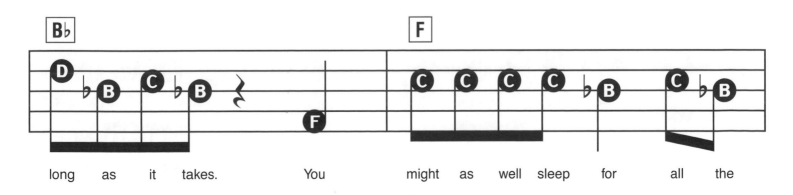

long as it takes. You might as well sleep for all the

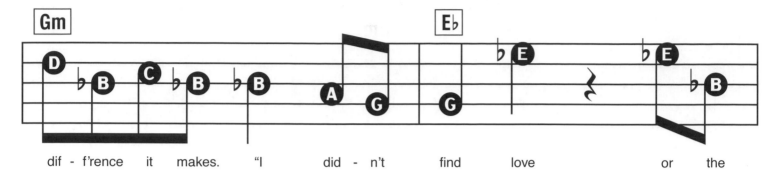

dif - f'rence it makes. "I did - n't find love or the

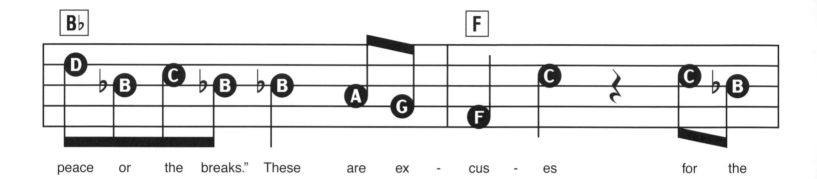

peace or the breaks." These are ex - cus - es for the

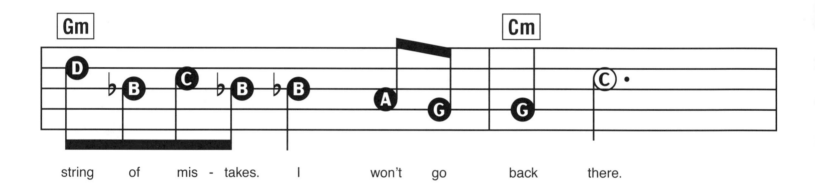

string of mis - takes. I won't go back there.

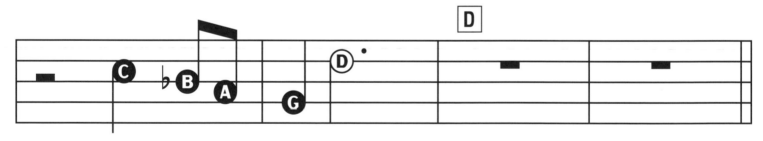

Not go - ing back there.

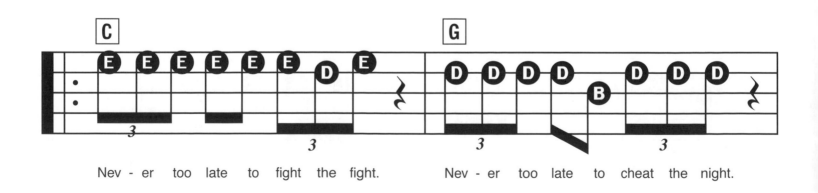

Nev - er too late to fight the fight. Nev - er too late to cheat the night.

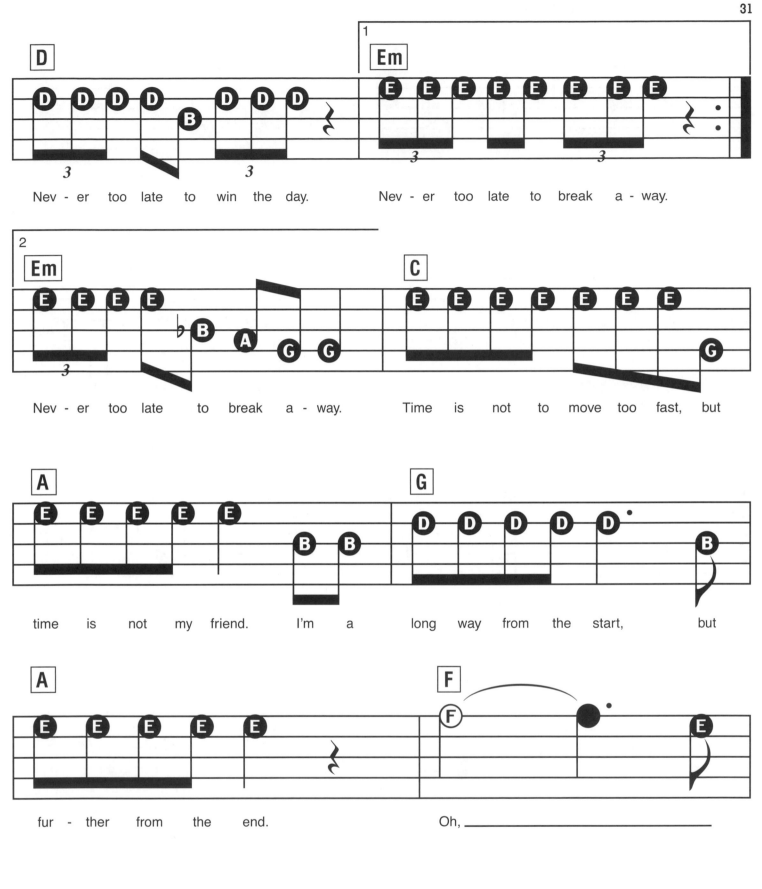

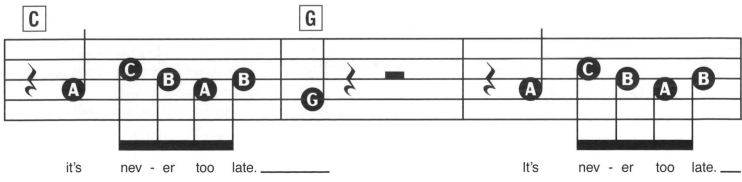

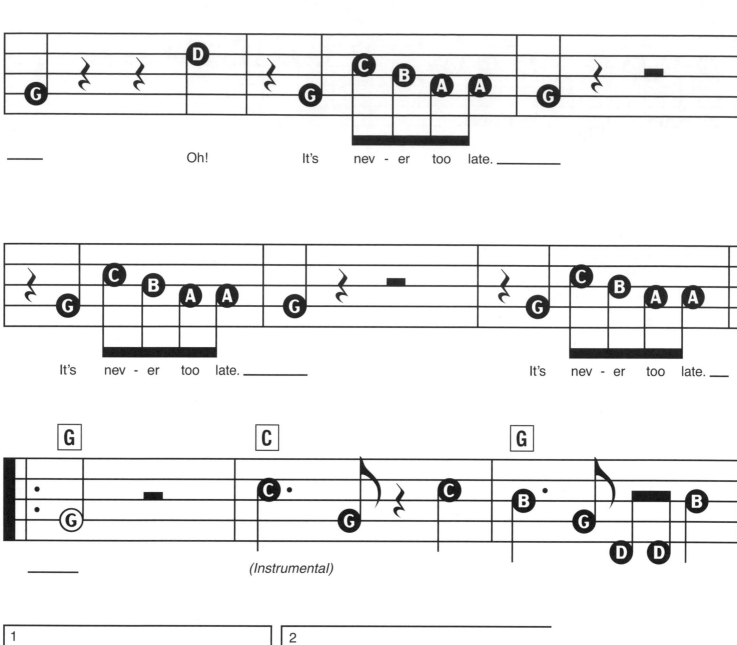

Oh! It's nev - er too late. _____

It's nev - er too late. _____ It's nev - er too late. __

(Instrumental)

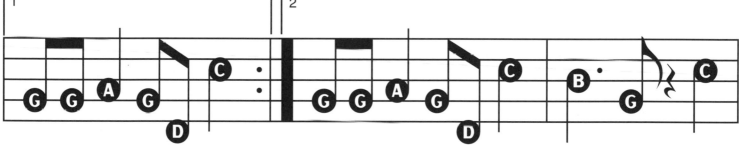

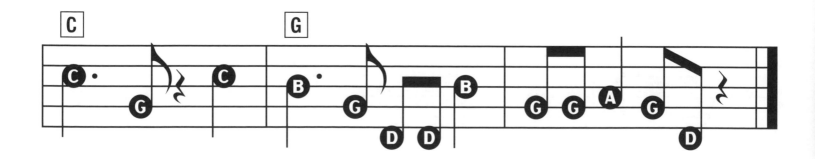

Spirit

Registration 2
Rhythm: Afro-Caribbean or Rock

Written by Timothy McKenzie,
Ilya Salmanzadeh and Beyoncè

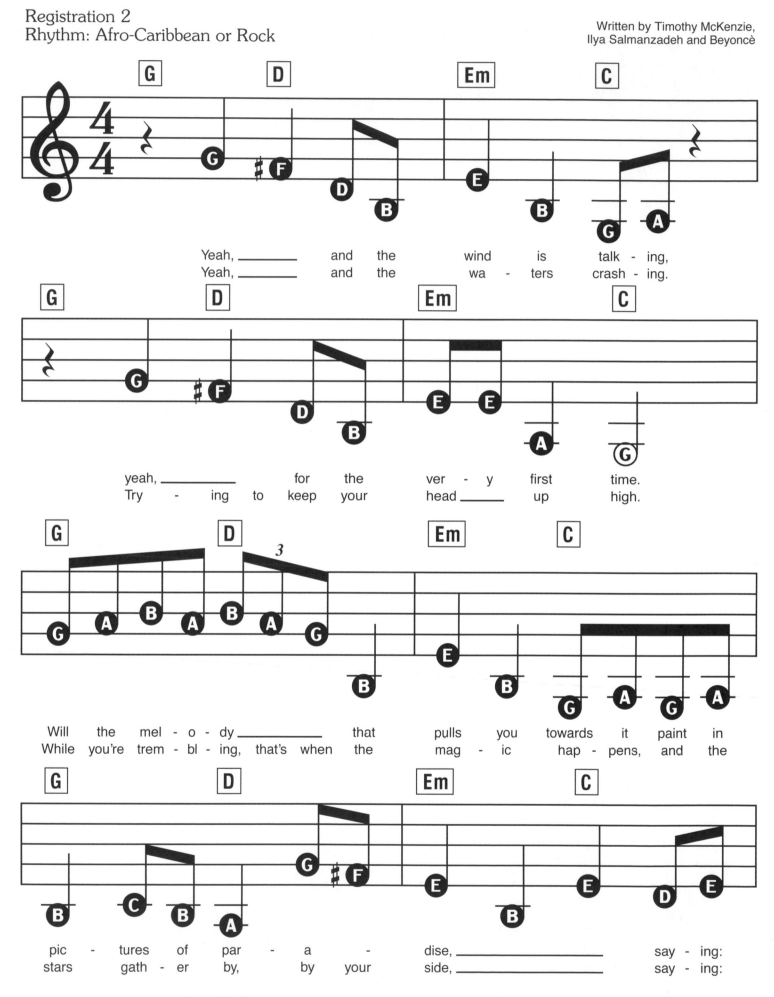

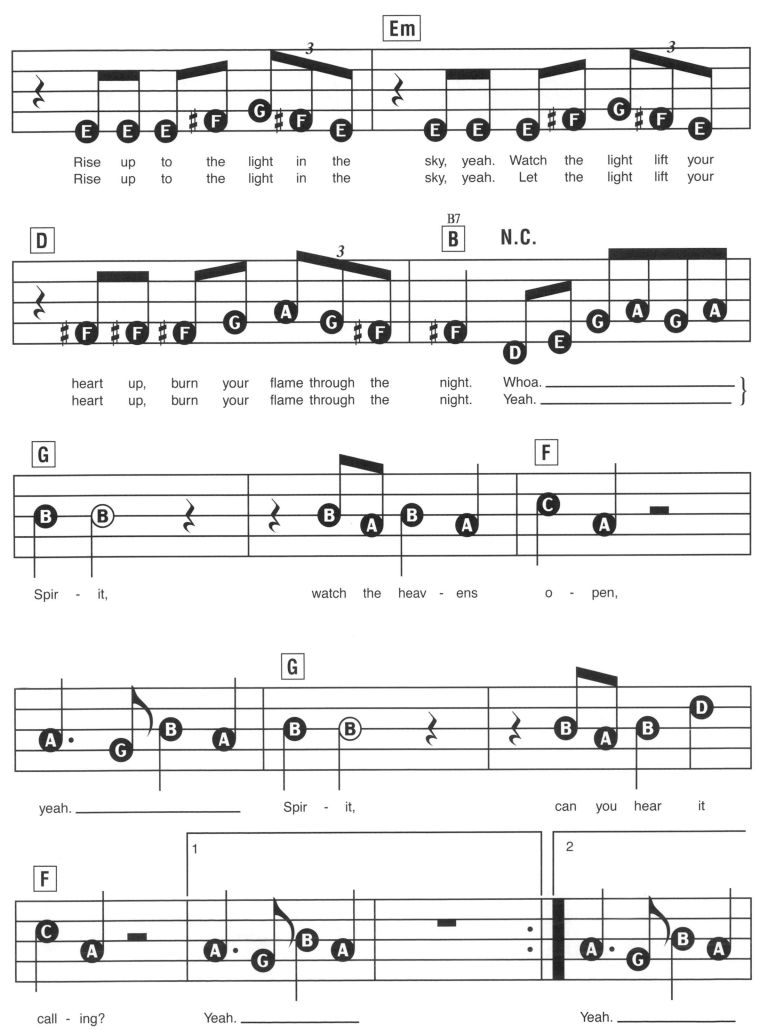

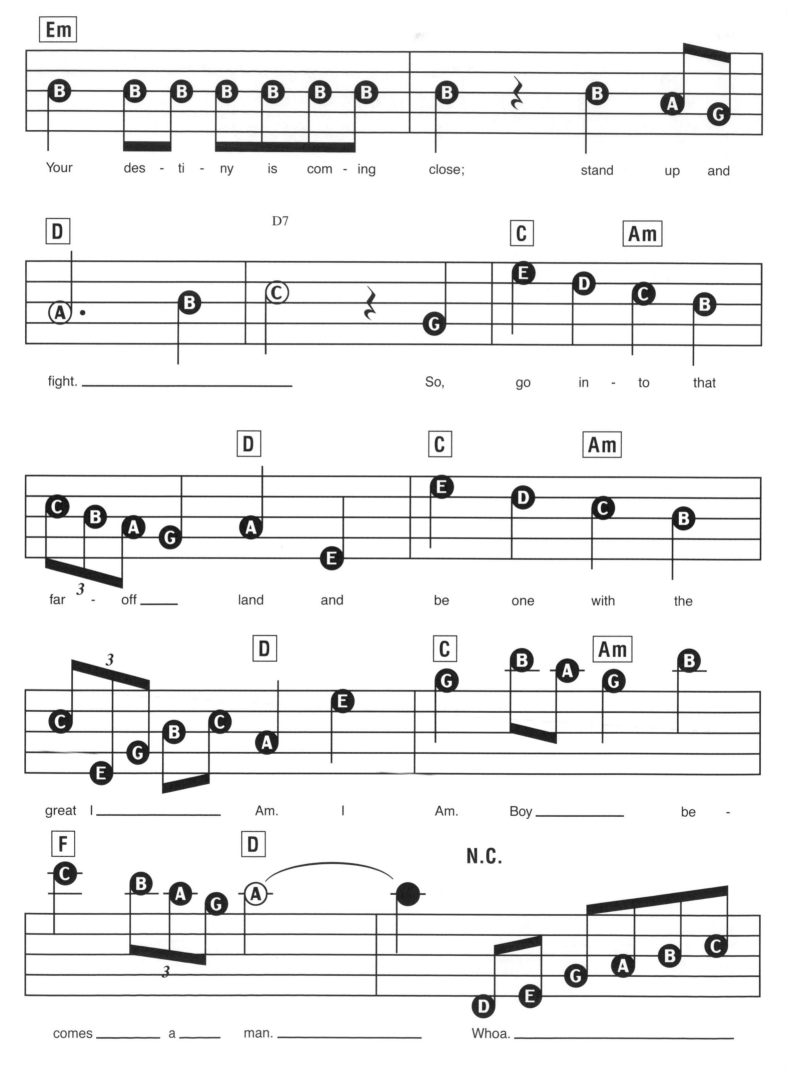

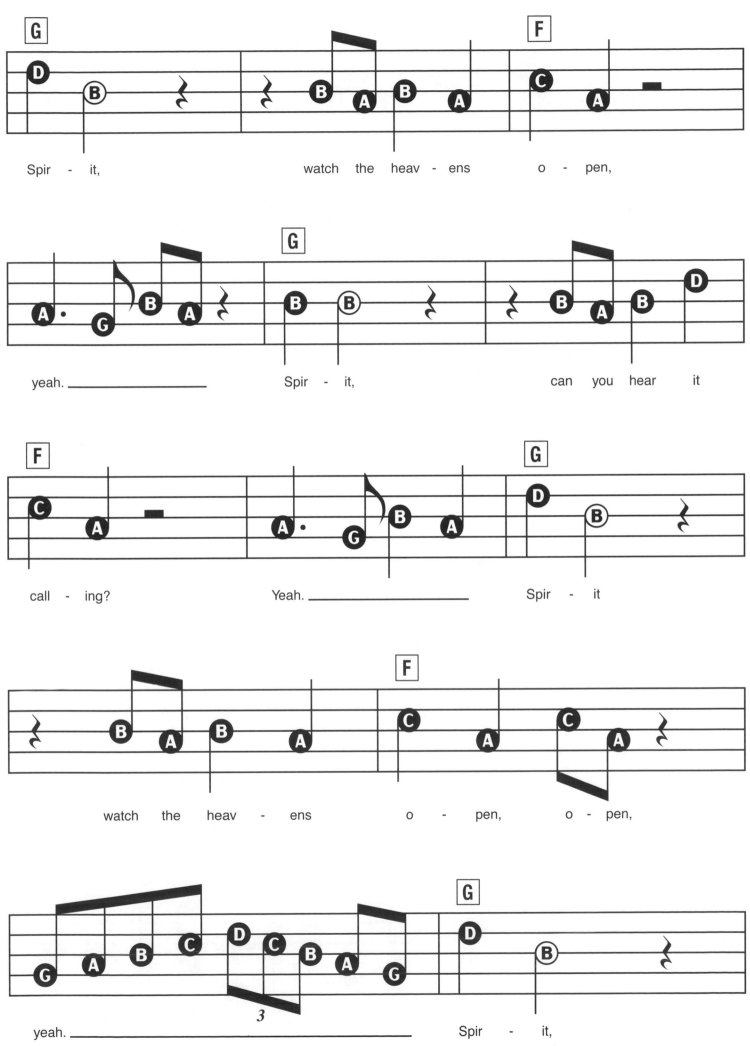

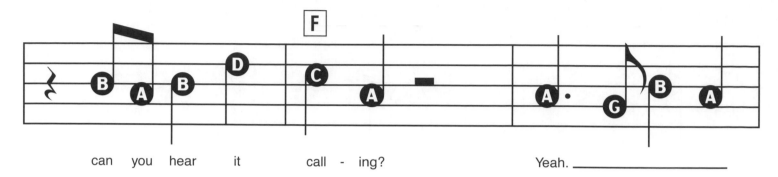

can you hear it call - ing?   Yeah. _____

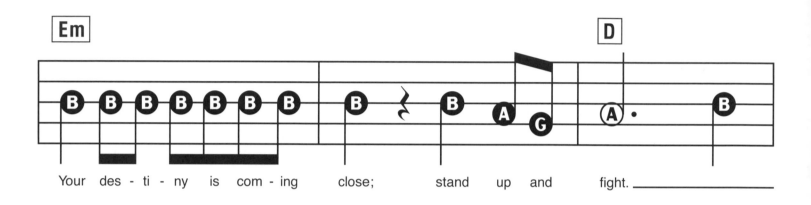

Your des - ti - ny is com - ing close;   stand up and fight. _____

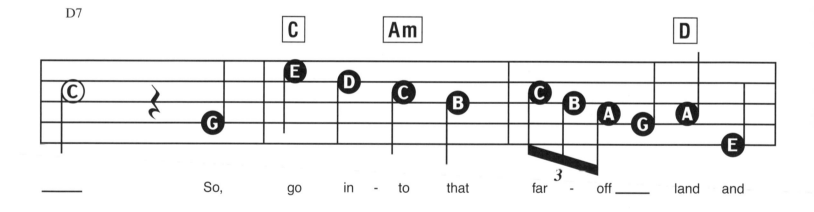

_____ So,   go in - to that   far - off ____ land and

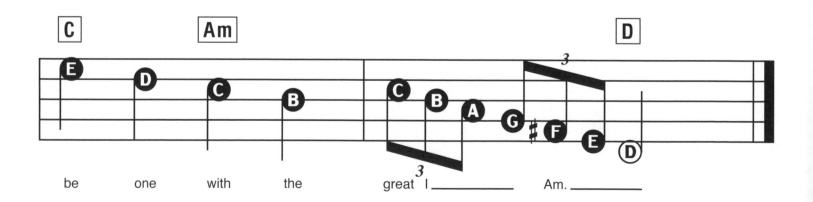

be one with the   great I _____   Am. _____

- Match the Registration number on the song to the corresponding numbered category below. Select and activate an instrumental sound available on your instrument.

- Choose an automatic rhythm appropriate to the mood and style of the song. (Consult your Owner's Guide for proper operation of automatic rhythm features.)

- Adjust the tempo and volume controls to comfortable settings.

Registration

1	Mellow	Flutes, Clarinet, Oboe, Flugel Horn, Trombone, French Horn, Organ Flutes
2	Ensemble	Brass Section, Sax Section, Wind Ensemble, Full Organ, Theater Organ
3	Strings	Violin, Viola, Cello, Fiddle, String Ensemble, Pizzicato, Organ Strings
4	Guitars	Acoustic/Electric Guitars, Banjo, Mandolin, Dulcimer, Ukulele, Hawaiian Guitar
5	Mallets	Vibraphone, Marimba, Xylophone, Steel Drums, Bells, Celesta, Chimes
6	Liturgical	Pipe Organ, Hand Bells, Vocal Ensemble, Choir, Organ Flutes
7	Bright	Saxophones, Trumpet, Mute Trumpet, Synth Leads, Jazz/Gospel Organs
8	Piano	Piano, Electric Piano, Honky Tonk Piano, Harpsichord, Clavi
9	Novelty	Melodic Percussion, Wah Trumpet, Synth, Whistle, Kazoo, Perc. Organ
10	Bellows	Accordion, French Accordion, Mussette, Harmonica, Pump Organ, Bagpipes